To Joshua
Happy Read

Belinda at Whiteways.
X

SUPERBASE 20

BADEN SÖLLINGEN

SUPERBASE 20

BADEN SÖLLINGEN

The Hornet's Nest

Chris Bennett

1 154537 00

OSPREY
AEROSPACE

For Captain Kirk Leuty

Published in 1991 by Osprey Publishing
Limited
59 Grosvenor Street, London W1X 9DA

© Chris Bennett

British Library Cataloguing in Publication
Data

Bennett, Chris
    Superbase 20 Baden Söllingen.
    1. Canada, Canadian Armed Forces
(Air).
    Aerodromes
    I. Title
    358. 4170943464

ISBN 0-85045-114-9

Editor Dennis Baldry
Page design David Tarbutt
Printed in Hong Kong

Front cover Each carrying a pair of
330 US gallon fuel tanks to maximize
their combat endurance, 'India
Flight', a formation of CF-18s from
No 421 TFS, perform an immaculate
positioning turn

Back cover Hornet pilot: the
lightweight HGU-55/P helmet—
standard issue in the USAF—has been
widely adopted by other NATO air
forces. Each '55 is custom made, the
interior being moulded to fit the
pilot's head. Comfort is important in
combat; the helmet's lightness helps
to reduce the strain on neck muscles
during high-G manoeuvres

Title page Capt Hart Prosch prepares
to tuck himself into the only other
resident jet type at Baden Söllingen—
one of the Base Flight's classic T-Birds

Right The author scans the sky from
the back seat of a CF-18B during a
photo-call with No 421 TFS

For a catalogue of all books published by Osprey Aerospace
please write to:

**The Marketing Manager, Consumer Catalogue Department
Osprey Publishing Ltd, 59 Grosvenor Street, London, W1X 9DA**

Introduction

Canadian Forces Base Baden Söllingen nestles in the shade of the Black Forest near the famous spa and casino town of Baden Baden in Germany. Under Canadian jurisdiction since 1953, the *'Kanadische Flugplatz'* is home to the happy aviators and ground crews of the 1st Canadian Air Division (1CAD), and its three constituent Tactical Fighter Squadrons: No 409 'Nighthawks' (blue squadron), No 421 'Red Indians' (red squadron) and No 439 'Sabre Toothed Tigers' (yellow squadron).

The 1st Canadian Air Division is responsible for the Canadian Armed Forces' principal contribution to NATO Allied Air Forces Central Europe, and all three CF-18 squadrons are tasked with both air superiority and ground attack roles. The pilots of 1CAD have built a considerable reputation within NATO for the way in which they exploit the hi-tech capabilities of the McDonnell Douglas CF-18.

A tour of duty on the CF-18 at CFB Baden Söllingen is generally recognized as being the plum posting for a fighter pilot in the Canadian Armed Forces (Air). Once there, the 'scam' is to find a legitimate reason to extend your stay. But few seem to succeed, as there is always a regular turn-around of name tags and personalized *bier steins* in the Officers' Mess.

All the personnel in 1CAD are keenly aware of their deterrent role within NATO and let everyone know that there are no points for second place. Equipped with what they consider to be the best jet in town, 1CAD continues a proud Canadian fighting tradition. This book is dedicated to the memory of Captain Kirk Leuty of No 439 TFS, whose life was snatched away during an airborne incident in April 1990. His tragic loss will long be remembered at CFB Baden Söllingen.

The author would like to offer his grateful thanks to everyone at CFB Baden Söllingen, without whose friendly and positive attitude this book would not have been possible. Special thanks are due to Lt Col John 'Baggy' Bagshaw, Lt Col Clive 'Cactus' Caton, Maj Brian 'BJ' Salmon, Capt Ric Berti, Capt Hart Prosch, Capt Chris 'Gloves' Glover, Capt Bob 'Cowboy' Painchaud, Capt Rick 'Redeye-Mongo-Transformer' Lloyd and Sqn Ldr Paul Day. Thanks also to Paul 'Wobbler' Waller of Harpers Photographic and John Pitchforth of Nikon UK Ltd.

All photo-imagery produced using Nikon F4 and F801 cameras equipped with Nikkor lenses and loaded with Kodachrome stock.

Contents

Blast from the past. This Canadair CF-104 Starfighter is a proud sentinel over the main road into CFB Baden Söllingen

Hornet blast-off

The pilot's left hand smoothly guides the throttle levers through the detent into full afterburner as his CF-18A devours JP-8 fuel in a profusion of noise and raw power

In common with all Hornets, the CF-18 packs a pair of General Electric F404 turbofans, each with a sea level rating of nearly 16,000 pounds of thrust with full augmentation (afterburner). At combat weight these potent powerplants give the jet a thrust-to-weight ratio better than unity, enabling the pilot to maintain acceleration in vertical manoeuvres

A deadly duo of 'double-juggers' thunder down the concrete in their quest for speed and flight. The term double-juggers is used to describe jets fitted with 330 US gallon external fuel tanks

Right Staining the sky with burnt JP-8, a pair of CF-18s make an urgent getaway. Vortices swirl from their wing tips as moisture is squeezed out of the humid summer air

The CF-18 is rotated at 155 knots on take-off, unsticking moments later at 170 knots. Using maximum dry thrust (military power, or MIL), the jet is accelerated to 350 KIAS (Knots Indicated Air Speed) at an angle of attack (AOA) of between 10 and 15 degrees until Mach 0.85 is established. When a full afterburner departure is required, the jet is capable of attaining 400 KIAS/Mach 0.9 in less than one minute from brakes off

Preceding spread With the prospect of some violent BFM (Basic Fighter Manoeuvres) on their minds, these battle hungry pilots from No 409 TFS 'Nighthawks' gain altitude over the Black Forest. Although these jets wear Nos 409 and 439 TFS idents on their tail fins, aircraft are rotated through all three squadrons as required and are therefore not necessarily operated by the unit whose badge they display

Right The same duo silhouetted against the dazzling sun, that age old friend and foe to the fighter pilot. The Hornet was selected as Canada's New Fighter Aircraft (NFA) in April 1980, the first of 138 aircraft (including 24 two-seaters), arriving in October 1982. Officially designated CF-188, abbreviated to CF-18A for the single-seater or CF-18B for the two-seater combat-capable trainer, the Hornet replaced the much loved CF-104 Starfighter and the rather less admired CF-5 Freedom Fighter in the strike/attack/reconnaissance role, and the truly awesome CF-101 Voodoo in the air defence role

Hornet's sting

The fuel hose injects 'motion lotion' as smartly attired ground crew proudly give their jet a final buff up before the pilot walks out. The name Hornet is not officially recognized by the Canadian Armed Forces (Air) because the word is not bilingual in English and French, but it would be unwise to emphasize this point around Baden Söllingen

Turn-around for a CF-18B outside its HAS (Hardened Aircraft Shelter), an imposing structure which seems to exemplify the motto of this front-line superbase: 'Auf Wacht' (On Guard)

Right An F404's view of the outside world through its simple, fixed-geometry jet intake

Below Thrust of the Hornet. Despite the fact that current fighter powerplants are exceptionally reliable, the Hornet's twin-engine configuration was probably the deciding factor in Canada's decision to buy the McDonnell Douglas product in preference to its single-engined arch-rival, the General Dynamics F-16 Fighting Falcon. The provision of a 'spare' engine is especially relevant to Hornet air defence patrols above Canada's vast tracts of inhospitable, featureless terrain, and the (feathered) FOD-laden skies of Europe. The closely spaced jet nozzles minimize thrust asymmetry in the event of power loss from either engine

In common with their airborne brethren, ground crews need regular and realistic practice in order to maintain operational efficiency. Secure inside a HAS, this blue-shirted crew from No 409 TFS utilize an otherwise redundant CF-18 to hone their re-arming skills against the clock. An inert AIM-7 Sparrow missile is quickly positioned on to Station Four, the port nacelle fuselage conformal . . .

. . . followed smartly by an LAU-5003 Multiple Rocket Launcher on Station Two, the port outboard. The LAU-5003 carries nineteen 2.75 inch rockets which can be fired either individually, or in salvo with 40 milliseconds separation. Inert or captive stores are normally painted over completely or, as here, partially blue

Red-shirted personnel from No 421 TFS prepare to download a weapons pylon off Station Two, port outboard. The Hornet can carry a wide variety of weaponry totalling over 7700 kg on nine stations, including a brace of AIM-9 Sidewinders on the wing tips. There are two outboard underwing stations for air-to-ground ordnance or additional AIM-7/-9 missiles; two inboard underwing stations for fuel tanks or more mud-moving ordnance; two conformal fuselage stations for AIM-7 Sparrows or sensor pods; and one station on the fuselage centreline which is usually occupied by a fuel tank. Twin and triple weapon ejection racks add even more versatility, and can be slung underwing carrying 500 lb bombs etc, as required

Sting of the Hornet. In common with a succession of US fighters dating back to the F-104A Starfighter, the fixed armament of the Hornet is the tried and combat tested M61A-1 Vulcan cannon. First fired in 1953, the M61 is a six-barrel 'Gatling' design of 20 mm calibre and is capable of firing 100 rounds per second. But as the weapon requires about 0.3 second to reach full operational firepower, the preferred short duration burst results in a slightly slower average rate of fire — which is just as well, because the magazine's capacity of 570 rounds would otherwise be expended in less than six seconds. Unlike other jet fighters, the Hornet has its cannon mounted in the nose along the centreline, an ideal location for absorbing recoil and virtually eliminating asymmetric fatigue loading to the airframe. To prevent the operation of the adjacent APG-65 radar being upset by shock and vibration, the radar unit is 'floated' on specially designed mounts which reduce the local G loading from 400 to 30 G when the cannon is fired

Capt Ric Berti of No 421 TFS, the 'Red Indians', pre-flights his jet under the protection of the thick blast-proof walls of the HAS before start-up. Unlike USAFE, Canadian Armed Forces Europe regulations dictate that all aircrew wear high-visibility life jackets. The jacket also connects the pilot, via a yellow lanyard, to a survival pack located in the seat pan of his Martin-Baker ejection seat

Right The Hornet utilizes Hands On Throttle And Stick (HOTAS) technology pioneered by the company's earlier F-15 Eagle, and Cathode Ray Tube (CRT) displays specially designed to minimize pilot workload, keeping the pilot's eyes out of the cockpit to maximize combat awarness and encourage the employment, rather than merely the operation, of the aircraft. Incorporating advanced digital technology, the cockpit environment is dominated by three large CRTs called Digital Display Indicators (DDIs). The left and right DDIs are interchangeable and, using any of the 20 grey push buttons surrounding each unit, the pilot can access a wealth of data, including systems status, checklists, engine performance and status, radar control and sensor information. The lower, central DDI, or Horizontal Indicator, is dedicated to navigational information and incorporates a Moving Map Display (MMD). At the heart of the avionics suite is the mission computer system—two digital computers with a core memory controllable via the centrally located Up Front Controller (UFC)

Right and far right Service with a smile—that's the philosophy of the 1 Air Maintenance Squadron (1AMS). Staffed by approximately 570 military personnel in addition to a number of local civilian employees, 1AMS is tasked with providing safe, fully operational aircraft for all three Tactical Fighter Squadrons in 1CAD

Below A 'Red Indian' jet receives first class turn-around treatment. Tell-tale carbon deposits around the cannon's gas vents indicate a recent visit to the gunnery range. Mounted on Station Eight is an SUU-20 training weapons dispenser, which is capable of carrying six practice bombs and four CRV-7 2.75 inch rockets

Below The previous Base Commander of CFB Baden Söllingen, General (formely Colonel) Jean Boyle, begins the complicated harness procedure required to ensconce himself in the jet before 'systems up'. Strapping into a fast jet is usually a time consuming exercise at first, even with assistance, but pilots experienced on type only seem to take a few seconds to sort out all the straps, buckles, sockets, clips and pins. General Boyle is currently Commander, Canadian Forces Europe, having moved 'down the road' to CFB Lahr. The vacated position of Base Commander at Baden Söllingen was filled by Colonel Keith McDonald

Hornet mission

Left A pilot from No 409 TFS 'Nighthawks' takes the first stride towards another demanding mission. The lightweight steps stow neatly into the port wing LEX (Leading Edge Extension). No 409 Sqn was formed in 1941 and initially operated the Boulton Paul Defiant before re-equipping with the Bristol Beaufighter and later the de Havilland Mosquito. The 'Nighthawks' earned their nickname during operations with the Allied Tactical Air Force, in which they became the command's highest scoring night fighter unit—exploits which inspired the squadron's motto: 'Midnight is our Noon'. Post-war, No 409 Sqn, Royal Canadian Air Force, was reformed in 1954 and simultaneously entered the jet age with the Avro Canada CF-100 'Clunk'. The squadron subsequently enjoyed an equally happy association with the mighty McDonnell CF-101 Voodoo until, in July 1984, it became the first operational squadron to receive the CF-18, transfering from CFB Cold Lake to Baden Söllingen a year later

Below Major Duffy Sullivan's face reveals the lasting impression of his oxygen mask as, having shut down and shed his harness, he unwinds both mentally and physically before egressing the jet. Duffy had just flown a particularly tough DACT (Dissimilar Air Combat Training) mission against F-15 Eagles from the 36th Tactical Fighter Wing, USAFE, at Bitburg. Operating one of the hottest jets in the European theatre, the boys from Baden are popular but potentially unforgiving and unrelenting DACT partners. The Hornets of 1CAD regularly work out with other NATO air forces for the mutual benefit of all concerned

Left A pilot from No 421 TFS receives the traditional 'thumbs up' from his red-capped crew chief in response to a fully operational graphite epoxy composite airbrake

Below Visually diffused by hot exhaust gases, a CF-18 taxies from dispersal en route for the 'last chance' area. The immensely strong landing gear of the Hornet was designed to absorb the punishment associated with carrier operations. The main wheels retract by folding rearwards and twisting through 90 degrees before tucking up into their wells to lie flat in the base of the intake ducts. Tyre pressures are 250 psi for the mains and 150 psi for the nose wheels — unless you're aviating a US Navy or Marine Corps F/A-18, in which case the main B F Goodrich tyres are inflated to a rock-hard 350 psi

Overleaf The pilot gives a cheery wave as he guides his CF-18B out of its HAS and emerges from behind a grass covered bunker. The 'Dual' is a fully operational Hornet, the only relevant penalty of the second seat being a small reduction in internal fuel capacity. Duals are primarily used to give new pilots check and orientation flights, but are also available for VIP rides

Below Lt Col John 'Baggy' Bagshaw in command of a CF-18B destined for a check flight in the late afternoon sunshine. Protruding from the nose gear leg is the catapult strop link for attaching the Hornet to the powerful steam catapults on US Navy carriers

Maj Brian 'BJ' Salmon, a pilot with No 421 TFS, eases his jet away from the hard stand. The small rigid stabilator attached to the LEX is a modification designed to divert boundary layer airflow away from the twin fins, which would otherwise vibrate excessively and cause unnecessary fatigue damage to the rest of the airframe, especially during sustained high AOA manoeuvers

Below Sitting snugly in his jet, and looking every inch the 'fighter pilot about town' (in HGU-55 helmet, light summer flight suit and matching kid leather gloves), Capt Chris 'Gloves' Glover of No 421 TFS exits the dispersal area. The CF-18 is equipped with a Martin-Baker SJU-9A zero/zero ejection seat which provides a reliable means of escape from a stricken jet at speeds up to 600 KIAS

Right 'Gloves' was elected to the post of Hornet demonstration pilot for the 1989 airshow season. This is a much sort after assignment for 'hero' fighter pilots, but one that is, make no mistake, highly demanding and exacting if the necessary safety standards are to be maintained

Things hot up as a pair of double-juggers give way to a Dual. Bound for the ranges, the jets are armed with SUU-20 training weapons dispensers. At this stage the dispensers still carry safety pins and high-visibility warning flags but, if the jets are 'good to go', these will be removed by ground crews during the 'last chance' checks before launch

Below A 'Nighthawk' taxies briskly en route to the active. The 600,000 candlepower quartz-halogen spotlight (clearly visible just above the nose gear doors) is unique to the CF-18 and was specified to enable nocturnal visual identification of intruding 'bogeys'. Reports of pilots allegedly using this light to simulate approaching UFOs remained unconfirmed as this book went to press

Overleaf Major Brian 'BJ' Salmon, one of the most knowledgeable and experienced air combat exponents at Baden Söllingen, heads out to the blue arena to tangle with fellow pilots from No 421 TFS. The generously proportioned laminated acrylic teardrop canopy gives the pilot excellent panoramic visibility from the cockpit—an uncluttered view of the sky is vital to enable small, elusive targets to be 'eyeballed' and tracked in a fast and furious dogfight. The pilot who sees his opponent first is usually the victor. 'BJ' began his air force career as a Voodoo navigator, which may explain his hilarious repertoire of true(?) stories—guaranteed to empty any bar within seconds. Seriously, 'BJ' helps to create the very best in Friday night Bier Calls

Below Landing roll: wing flaps at 45 degrees and ailerons drooped to 42 provide extra drag to assist deceleration and braking effect

Below right The Hornet's advanced digital 'fly by wire' system is responsible for all aspects of flight control via the Flight Control Computer (FCC). The FCC digitally interprets inputs from the pilot's conventional flight controls and converts them electronically into optimum manoeuvre commands to the relevant control surfaces. This system enables the pilot to fly the jet to the outer limits of its performance envelope with the minimum risk of departing from controlled flight—a big confidence builder which encourages aggressive combat manoeuvres

Overleaf A 'Nighthawk' taxies towards the holding point for Runway 21 as another 'Hawk takes off in afterburner, leaving a cone of scorching jet exhaust in its wake. Thanks to General Electric, the Hornet has plenty of thrust in hand, the majority of take-offs from the main 8128-ft runway being easily accomplished in Military Power, saving a considerable amount of fuel. In the case of a full afterburner take-off, great care must be taken to retract the landing gear immediately after a positive rate of climb is established in order to avoid an embarrassing 'sudden twang'; it also helps to cut down the paperwork if the pilot monitors the jet's AOA to prevent a supersonic transition during the climb out. If full afterburner is maintained on departure, it's possible to reef into a near vertical climb (80 degrees AOA to be exact) and reach an altitude of over 40,000 ft in less than 2.5 minutes from brakes off

Hornet healers

Right Appropriately attired ground crew carefully prepare to trundle a jet off to the 'doctors' for some routine maintenance

Following spread In the scrupulously clean confines of the 'hospital', more brightly dressed personnel quickly begin the serious business of ensuring the Hornet's longevity

Graphite epoxy composites cover some 40 per cent of the Hornet's surface area, but only account for ten per cent of airframe weight. Extremely strong and corrosion resistant, composite materials are used for the wing skins, trailing edge flaps, ailerons, vertical fins and tailerons; also for the horizontal stabilators, airbrake and landing gear doors

51

To the relief of all concerned, the Hornet is a reliable and easily maintainable combat aircraft. Utilizing a total of 307 conveniently placed access doors, and equipped with easily transferable Line Replaceable Units (LRUs), the jet's a joy to work on; minor avionic problems can usually be solved with the minimum of hassle

A General Electric F404-GE-400 turbofan is lowered on to a dolly for transportation to the 'hush house', where a thorough diagnostic appraisal of the powerplant is undertaken before repair or regular maintenance. Engine changes are usually necessary either for major remedial work, or when one of the component modules has reached the end of its scheduled life. The F404 measures a tad over 13-ft long and weighs 2120-lb complete with accessories. The slick Hornet healers at Baden Söllingen can remove and replace an F404 in less than 30 minutes, aided somewhat by only having to deal with ten connections between engine and airframe

The performance of an F404 is safely monitored from the control room as an idle to afterburner acceleration test is performed within the hush house

The hush house incorporates the latest in performance and diagnostic evaluation equipment. Problem areas are isolated without having to tear the engine apart, and removal rates are kept to a minimum. The engine test rig can easily be dismantled to allow the hush house to accommodate an entire aircraft for engine runs if required, usually to establish whether engine removal is desirable

Working at the jet wash. The skies around Baden Söllingen are often badly affected by airborne pollution, so the wash house attracts a queue of regular customers. Although the accumulation of muck has a negligible effect on flight performance and arguably improves the camouflage effect of the matt tactical grey paint scheme, it's considered to be decidedly uncool to dogfight in a dirty jet

Base Flight: T-Birds forever

Left One of Base Flight's T-Birds is removed from its shelter ready for another hard day's work. The 1st Canadian Air Division at Baden Söllingen continue to operate four CT-133ANs, the Canadair version of the most successful jet trainer in the Western world—the Lockheed T-33 Shooting Star. Known officially as the Silver Star, but unofficially as the good old T-Bird, Base Flight's aircraft are used extensively for high speed liason duties, aircrew proficiency flights and occasionally as radar or eyeball targets for CF-18s during BFM exercises

Below Accompanied by a fuel bowser and two examples of the most common and practical of on base transportation, a T-Bird waits for its midday top up

Bottom Fill her up, please. Unleaded? No thanks, just plain old honest to goodness JP-8 (NATO F-34)

Below Capt Hart Prosch, complete with obligatory Ray-Bans, proceeds to open the canopy of his trusty T-Bird before performing a thorough pre-flight walk around. If he had his uncomfortable, old-style parachute harness already fastened, it would be almost impossible for him to stand upright; these straps will therefore be left undone until he is ready to climb into the cockpit

Left Engine inlet covers removed, parachute now correctly slung and Ray-Bans stowed, Capt Prosch is ready to ride. Boarding the T-33, particularly for the rear seat occupant, requires (due to bulk of 'chute and angle of canopy) some practice to conduct in true 'casual' fighter pilot fashion. Capt Prosch subsequently transferred to CFB Cold Lake in order to complete his Fighter Pilot Course, which involves a five month induction period on the CF-5 Freedom Fighter before performing a six month conversion course on the CF-18 with No 410 Operational Training Squadron, the 'Cougars'

Below T-Bird '094 casts a star-shaped shadow over Runway 21 as it unsticks in unison with '052 to act as interception targets for a pair of CF-18s. The Silver Star was originally armed with two nose-mounted .50 calibre Browning M3 machine guns, but these were removed and the gun ports faired over some years ago. The front seater sports the current HGU-55 flying helmet, whereas the Guy In Black (GIB) evidently prefers a 'bone dome' of an earlier vintage

Preceding spread From 1952 until 1959, Canadair constructed a total of 656 Silver Stars under licence from Lockheed. Unlike the standard T-33 (powered by the Allison J33), the Canadair T-Bird features the slightly more punchy Rolls-Royce Nene turbojet, which has a sea level thrust rating of 5100 lb. The T-Bird is quite a speedster, being capable of 450 KIAS 'on the deck' and 200 KIAS at 25,000 ft

Right A pair of T-Birds run past the picturesque Hohenzollern Schloss in Bavaria, a favourite backdrop for air-to-air photography

Below The Rhine meanders peacefully below as T-Bird '094 rolls away from sistership '345. When the Royal Canadian Air Force was consolidated into the Canadian Armed Forces in 1968, the Silver Star was designated CT-133, often abbreviated to CT-33. New serial numbers were issued which all begin with '133' (eg 133094)

The Silver Star was aptly named, as most of the original fleet glistened in highly polished natural metal—so highly polished that in some cases much of the aircraft's remaining fatigue life was literally worn away! Base Flight's T-Birds still manage to look smart despite their tactical camouflage

Right Dressed in HGU-55 helmet, life jacket and USAF-issue flight suit, the author captured this self-portrait from the back seat of a Silver Star. Canada intends to operate this beautiful jet until the dawn of the 21st Century

Hornet handlers: 'Hawks, Indians & Tigers'

Left Capt Chris 'Gloves' Glover observes the performances of his fellow display pilots at Mildenhall's Air Fete '89

Above As his slot time approaches, Capt Glover prepares to display the CF-18 Hornet in front of an eager audience of more than 100,000 people. In common with every other aspect of the apparently glamorous life of the military aviator, display flying demands a substantial injection of practice time and nothing less than total professionalism. Once perfected, 'Gloves' flew his display sequence in front of the Base Commander, who had to approve the content, technique and, most importantly, safety of the performance

Lieutenant (now Captain) Ric Berti of No 421 TFS, the 'Red Indians', waits for his crew to present the steps before dismounting. In common with pilots in other NATO air forces, most of 1CAD's CF-18 pilots have secondary squadron duties. One of Ric's is the creative but somewhat sadistic role of 'Yogi Master'. Whenever a new intake of pilots is assigned to the 'Red Indians' — no matter whether they're young or not so young, innocent or experienced — they have to face the dreaded, age old ritual of the 'Making of the Brave'. This involves three trials: *'Trial by fire'*, the smoking of the pipe of peace, which is loaded with combustibles of a distinctly non-tobacco nature and guaranteed to make even the most trained fighter pilot's stomach rather unstable; *'Trial by Water'* simply involves the intake of an unspecified number of the wondrous and magical Yogi cocktail until suitably lubricated (simply to get the poor, unsuspecting initiate into a partying mood, you understand); and lastly *'Trial by Sport'*, involving direct participation in several traditional fighter pilot games — punctuated with the occasional, additional Yogi. If the would-be fighter pilot survives to tell the tale he can proudly proclaim himself a true 'Red Indian'

The Yogi, produced of a secret formula handed down through the ages and known only to the 'Yogi Master', is a potentially explosive concoction which even the most seasoned of Friday night Bier Callers has learned to respect. Never mind, it's down the hatch to the enthusiastic war cry of 421's happy tribe, *'Hi Ziggy Zumba'*!

A content Capt Ric Berti relaxes after a navigation exercise on a particularly hot and balmy day. Baden Söllingen is an extremely popular posting, so after a tour of duty is completed, and the almost inevitable order of transfer to Cold Lake, Moose Jaw, Bagotville or wherever arrives, it is initially met with a distinct lack of enthusiasm . . .

. . . a contemplation that Capt Hart Prosch, T-Bird pilot with Base Flight, knows only too well. But Capt Prosch, due to transfer through to CFB Cold Lake, had one consoling thought: *'In less than a year I could be back here as a regular CF-18 pilot!'*

Armed with *U-matic* video tape, chart and assorted publications, Maj Duffy Sullivan tackles the short stroll back to No 421's hardened bunker for debrief. Formed at Digby, Lincolnshire in 1942, No 421 Sqn won acclaim flying Spitfires from Kenley, the famous Battle of Britain aerodrome in Kent. During the Normandy invasion, the squadron switched from patrols and fighter sweeps to ground attack, moving across Europe until it disbanded at Utersen, Germany in July 1945. After it reformed in 1949 as part of the RCAF, No 421 Sqn operated de Havilland Vampire jet fighters from Chatham, New Brunswick and later RAF Odiham in Hampshire, England. Re-equipped with the Canadair Sabre Mk 5 in 1951, the squadron moved to Grostenquin in France and remained there until, in 1963, it converted to the Canadair CF-104 Starfighter and deployed to Baden Söllingen in the low-level, all-weather strike role in February 1964. After 22 years mounted on the CF-104, the 'Red Indians' received their first CF-18 in the spring of 1986

Capt Chris 'Gloves' Glover gives the 'heads up' to fellow 'Red Indian' pilot Capt Sean 'Burner' Byrne

Maj Pierre 'Dez' Desbiens offers a serious stare as he and 'Yogi Master' Ric Berti demonstrate that flying jet fighters isn't all there is to flying jet fighters. Each and every hop generates a surprising amount of paperwork which has to be shuffled both pre- and post-flight

A typical fighter pilot's day begins at 07.00 hours with the collective squadron Met briefing, followed by a recognition quiz and 'Emergency of the day' — a detailed review of one of the Hornet's galaxy of systems, and what to do (and what *not* to do) in the event of a malfunction. Depending on the scheduled take-off time, mission planning either precedes or follows a hearty breakfast. Mission planning includes a thorough overview of the sortie and takes account of every conceivable contingency in the event of fuel problems, radar failure, etc. Pilots need to be good navigators for obvious reasons, but they must also monitor their exact geographical position as it's all too easy to cause a little noise in the wrong area and upset the delicate PR balance which exists between their foreign military presence and the local (and sometimes vocal) civilian population

After mission planning and a meticulous pre-flight walk around inside the HAS, Capt Rob 'Juice' Jones clutches his USAF issue helmet bag as he climbs into the cockpit

Proudly sporting his No 421 TFS baseball cap, the intrepid Lt Col John 'Baggy' Bagshaw is offered a little assistance in the securing of his harness. Lt Col Bagshaw probably holds the all-time record for the highest zoom climb ever achieved in a Canadair Starfighter. During a routine air test, 'Baggy' explored the CF-104's flight envelope rather too enthusiastically; after accelerating to Mach 2.1 at medium altitude, he pitched the nose of the jet to 60 degrees above the horizon—by the time he had reached 85,000 ft it was becoming quite dark outside and the newly overhauled J79 engine didn't want to play anymore. At this point 'Baggy' decided to roll the jet inverted and pull through the vertical until he had descended to less rarified altitudes. But nothing happened. After losing control at zero airspeed and enduring an extremely high rate of descent (during which the engine could have easily flamed out), he recovered to straight and level flight at 30,000 ft. 'Baggy' readily admits that the patron saint of adventurous aviators must have been sitting on his shoulder that particular day

Below left After his last flight as Squadron Commander of No 421 TFS, Lt Col Bagshaw runs the gauntlet of the traditional aqueous attack before an enforced retreat to the *Bierhaus*. 'Baggy', who later transferred his Big Chief's headress on to the capable cranium of Lt Col Clive 'Cactus' Caton, remains at Baden Söllingen as Wing Operations Officer

Left Lt Col Bagshaw, Big Chief of the 'Red Indians', intimidates the photographer from behind the Squadron Commander's desk. Under his leadership, No 421 TFS has established an enviable reputation for operational efficiency. Lt Col Bagshaw is deservedly one of the most respected and admired commander's in the squadron's history

Below The partially personalized flying helmet of Guiseppe, a pilot from No 409 TFS

Overleaf A 'Nighthawk' kind of welcome

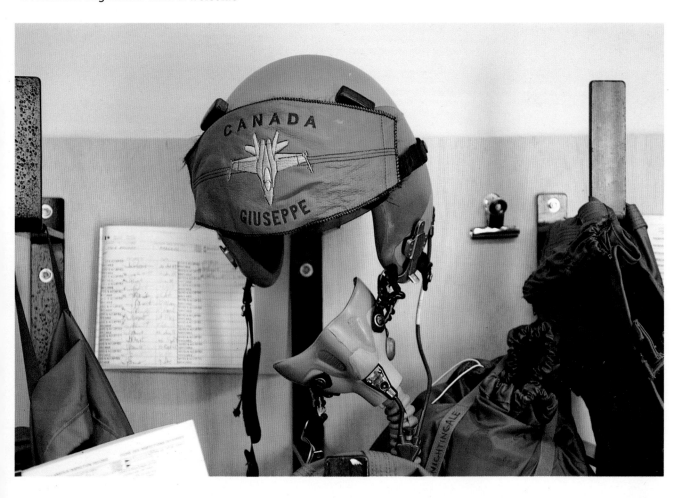

Hornet supreme

Major Brian 'BJ' Salmon, intent on some 'turning and burning', taxies past his No 2, Capt Ric Berti, in typical English weather at RAF Mildenhall in Suffolk

Left *4-2-1 Go!* 'BJ' Salmon stokes up his '404s into MIL, hurtling forwards to break the surly bonds. During the take-off roll the twin rudders are programmed to move inwards, thereby imparting greater downforce on the tail and enabling rotation to be achieved at lower speeds

Below left Nosewheel steering is used to maintain directional control on the runway until, at 155 knots, smooth aft stick pressure is applied to establish seven degrees AOA (Alpha). Once the Hornet is airborne and the gear retracted, this Alpha value is maintained until 350 knots; at this point the jet may be pitched to 10-15 degrees Alpha with reference to the velocity vector bug on the head-up display (HUD)

Below Hornet the hunter: dismal weather does not deter an aggressive fighter pilot

In combat, pilots are not interested in simply enjoying the view; they are much more concerned with . . .

. . . 'checksixability'

Preceding spread The Canadian Armed Forces (Air) took delivery of its 138th and last CF-18 in September 1988, over eight years after the Hornet purchase was announced in the Canadian Parliament

Below Clearly visible on the fins, aft fuselage and nose are the night formation strip lights which act as visual references for safe station keeping by emitting easily recognizable patterns according to relative formation position

Below Close formation flying has always been associated with fighter operations. No 439 Sqn arrived at Bournemouth, England in December 1943. Mounted on the Hawker Hurricane Mk IV and later Typhoon, the squadron wreaked havoc in the fighter bomber role during the Normandy campaign of 1944. Thirteen pilots had been awarded the Distinguished Flying Cross by the time the squadron had finished leap-frogging across Europe in support of the Allied advance into Germany. The squadron's inevitable post-war disbandment lasted until 1951, when they received the Canadair Sabre at Uplands in Ottawa before moving back across the Atlantic to RAF North Luffenham in England. During their stay at Marville in France, the 'Tigers' relinquished their trusty Sabre Mk 6s and re-equipped with the Canadair CF-104 Starfighter in March 1964, transferring to Baden Söllingen in July 1970 after a three-year posting to CFB Lahr. After 20 years of attack/reconnaissance operations with the CF-104, the squadron disbanded, but soon returned to the fighter business when, after a successful work-up with their new Hornets at CFB Cold Lake, the 'Tigers' roared back to Baden Söllingen in November 1985

Overleaf Apart from being compatible with the LAU-5003 rocket system, having a revised ILS (Instrument Landing System) and spotlight, the CF-18B two-seater is virtually identical to the F/A-18B combat-capable trainer operated by the US Navy and Marine Corps. The first Hornet two-seater, originally designated TF/A-18A, made its maiden flight in 1979

Preceding spread Two-plus-two: a pair of CF-18Bs make a formation recovery to base, ever alert to the threat of a sneaky 'bounce' by other fighters

Sharp formation breaks are one of the hallmarks of a front-line fighter squadron

Left Lt Col John 'Baggy' Bagshaw
rarely enjoys flying straight and
level . . .

. . . so time for a gentle wing over to
reveal the false canopy under the
forward fuselage. The Canadian
Armed Forces pioneered this
cunning con-trick, which disguises
the Hornet's direction of turn as much
as possible during visual combat
manoeuvres. One second of
confusion in the mind of an opposing
pilot is often enough to bring cannon
or Sidewinder to bear. He who
hesitates . . .

Right Vapour pouring from the LEX, Capt Chris 'Gloves' Glover demonstrates the Hornet's agility by snapping into a vertical climb. The leading edge extensions are designed to act as vortex generators, scrubbing the aerofoil clean of unwanted, slow moving air in the boundary layer. The LEX also increase maximum lift by 50 per cent, enabling controlled flight to be maintained at spectacularly high angles of attack (degrees Alpha). In addition the LEX also function as a compression wedge to reduce both the Mach Number and variation of airflow angle into the jet intakes throughout the flight envelope

Below Manoeuvring in the TRA (Temporary Reserved Airspace), Capt Glover initiates a high-G turn towards a 12 o'clock sun — a defensive combat option which may succeed in breaking the opposing pilot's visual track and make accurate weapon aiming more difficult

Left 'Burners and vapour as Capt Glover maintains energy during another accomplished demonstration of the CF-18s aerobatic (and combat) capabilities

Below 'Gloves' knife edges his Hornet to display the jet intakes under the wings, where they help to minimize the aircraft's radar cross-section (RCS)

Above With full flap augmented by fully depressed ailerons, a Hornet smokes the Goodriches as it arrives in characteristically naval fashion. As in the case of a carrier landing, the jet is not flared in the traditional manner but is literally flown on to the runway at a constant approach speed and angle of attack, though at a somewhat lower rate of descent. Compression of the main gear oleo struts closes a weight-on-wheels microswitch which signals the Flight Control Computer to transfer to ground mode

Top right A 'Tiger' jet established at eight degrees Alpha and 135 knots prepares to make contact with the concrete. Clearly visible in the foreground is the arrestor cable used for emergency 'trapping' in the event of brake or engine failure. Should this violent form of retardation prove necessary the Hornet is, of course, fitted with a tailhook as standard

Right With horizontal stabilators at full upwards deflection and rudders converging to create speed-reducing extra drag, a CF-18 make full use of the available runway to minimize brake wear. The large horizontal stabs function conventionally for pitch control of differentially for roll control, augmenting the ailerons

Hornet formation, Indian style

Right 'India's' One, Two, Three and Four overfly their nest, inbound from a hectic BFM exercise

Below Lt Col John 'Baggy' Bagshaw (leader), Lt Col Dave 'Bart' Bartram, Maj Brian 'BJ' Salmon and Capt Wes 'Sunny' Pshebylo—alias 'India Flight'—recall the unforgettable days of the 'Tiger Romeos', 1CAD's Starfighter-mounted demonstration team, which sadly did not survive into the Hornet era

Preceding spread The dynamic Lt Col Bagshaw calls for a formation change over a particularly healthy clump of Bavarian forest en route to . . .

Below . . . the noble edifice of Hohenzollern Schloss; one cannot help but hope that the castle's residents appreciate the number of free airshows they receive each year

Right Carefully avoiding their jet wake, Capt Bob 'Cowboy' Painchaud slips the camera ship underneath the formation. The pilots of 1CAD have evidently lost none of their skill in close, multi-ship formation flying despite the operational necessity of concentrating on widely spaced, two-ship combat elements

Bottom right The CF-18's tactical grey camouflage scheme performs a surprisingly good job of blending the formation into a typical rural town

Right Currently, the Hornet is only operated by Canada and Spain in European skies, but McDonnell Douglas sales persons continue to woo the German *Luftwaffe* with the Hornet 2000

Below 'Echelon port, go!' India Flight moves into tight formation as clouds hug the snow-capped Allgaver Alps on the German-Austrian border

Opposite page India Flight: One, Two, Three and Four tally India Five's six o'clock and demonstrate the outstanding rear-hemisphere visibility from the Hornet's spacious cockpit

Preceding spread Toting a high-visibility Captive Air Training Missle (CATM), India Four maintains close formation. The day-glow painted CATM is a peacetime concession to flight safety which makes the CF-18 more visible to civilian traffic and helps to reduce the risk of collision between opposing jets during air combat training

These pages and overleaf India break: after presenting three fingers to visually confirm the three second interval between the initiation of each jet's rolling manoeuvre, Lt Col Bagshaw leads off ... followed in sequence by India's Two, Three and Four

Hornet historic flight

Above Hornet meets Spitfire to commemorate No 421 Sqn's association with Britain's most famous fighter during World War 2

Right Sqn Ldr Paul Day pilots the RAF Battle of Britain Memorial Flight's Spitfire Mk XIX PS853, and Maj Brian 'BJ' Salmon the CF-18, as Capt Ric Berti places the photo ship into the ideal vantage point to capture the formation overflying the beach near Eastbourne in Sussex

Left The flight levels out in front of a Channel cliff face in much the same way as pursuing fighters must have done during the Battle of Britain fifty years earlier

Below Leading-edge slats and trailing-edge flaps partially extended, the Hornet maintains station on the Spitfire at a comfortable 250 knots. Sqn Ldr Paul Day has accumulated some 800 hours on the Hurricane and Spitfire since he joined the BBMF in 1980. The BBMF shares RAF Coningsby in Lincolnshire with the Tornado fighters of No 229 Operational Conversion Unit. As as instructor with No 229 OCU, Sqn Ldr Paul Day is conveniently placed to offer his services to the BBMF; he has amassed over 5000 hours on fast jets, mostly on the F-4 Phantom II, but more recently on the Tornado Air Defence Variant

Overleaf Spitfire PS853 is the most recent addition to the BBFM's impressive fleet (which includes two Hurricanes, six Spitfires and a Lancaster), and last saw RAF service with the Woodvale Met Flight in 1957. Powered by a specially modified Rolls-Royce Griffon 58 from an Avro Shackleton, the Spitfire is painted in the overall blue scheme used by RAF photo-reconnaissance aircraft. Interestingly, the BBFM's Lancaster bomber (a direct descendant of the Shackleton), is no longer the world's only airworthy example. Thanks to the magnificent efforts of Canadian Warplane Heritage, their Lancaster Mk X FM213 flew again in the summer of 1988

The Spitfire was, and is, a near-
perfect blend of form and function, a
combination of qualities which few
other fighter designs have been able
to equal, even now